Creating A Successful Meetup Group

A Business Building Tool for Aromatherapists

MANDY SAVARD

DISCLAIMER

Meetup, Inc. has no affiliation with this guide and is not responsible for its content. For official Meetup recommendations/questions/forums/blogs, please go to http://www.meetup.com/help . Certain features and the design of Meetup's website may have been added, revised or removed since this publication, and therefore the specific Information in this guide may not be directly applicable to the features or design of the current website. The Meetup name and logo and other related trademarks are the property of Meetup, Inc. The Clinical Alchemy name, Logo and other related trademarks are the property of Clinical Alchemy.

Copyright -

To contact the author for inquiries about speaking engagements, consulting, or bringing business education to your establishment please email Clinical Alchemy at Info@aromacoaching.com

Creating A Successful Meetup Group – A Business Building Tool for Aromatherapists

PUBLISHER'S NOTE

Published May 2014
Self-Published using CreateSpace

Dear Aromatherapists,

First and foremost, thank you for purchasing this Guide! So many people have great ideas but they don't take action. Congratulations on taking that first step! The Aromatherapy Industry can be very challenging but also very rewarding.

While studying to become a Certified Clinical Aromatherapist I was so caught up in learning the ins and outs of essential oils and proper usage that I did not realize, until I was finished, that there was only one chapter in my studies dedicated to Business! It was not the fault of my instructor, it just is not something that seems to be covered across the board. I was Certified, I am good at what I do, so where were all my clients??!!??

Sound familiar? Fortunately, before becoming a Certified Clinical Aromatherapist I completed a Bachelor's Degree in Business Management and a Master's Degree in Organizational Leadership. Now, a lot of learning later, I have found the perfect marriage between my love of all things Aromatherapy and my love of all things business.

Here's the great part for you. I have already weeded through that jungle so that YOU don't have to experience the time consuming struggle that I went through. You will be able to get right down to business creating your successful Meetup Group.

This book is designed to be a guide for you to utilize during your journey to building a thriving Aromatherapy Meetup Group. Work at your own pace and remember that sometimes a slow start to a new group can be the best start.

Best Wishes,

Mandy

Mandy Savard
Certified Clinical Aromatherapist, Business Development Coach
Owner, Clinical Alchemy http://www.clinicalalchemy.com
Follow me on Twitter: @AromaCoachMandy and
Follow me on Facebook: www.facebook.com/aromacoachmandy

MANDY SAVARD

CONTENTS

ACKNOWLEDGMENTS

Thank you so much to my Mentor, Sue, for all of her encouragement and wisdom that she has given me through my journey as an Aromatherapist and thank you to my husband to be for encouraging me in business endeavors every step of the way.

1 WHY START A MEETUP GROUP

Meetup.com can be a great resource, as an Aromatherapist, to educate, build a community, and possibly increase your business sales – IF done right. I co-run a successful Meetup Group in my area that has grown each month while creating a sense of community within our core group members. As a perk, business has been gained from this Meetup group WITHOUT PUSHING SALES OR ASKING FOR SALES.

How is that, you ask? Our Meetup group members trust us and our information. Several of our group members have told us that they were hesitant to join because they had been tricked into sitting through several essential oil sales pitches that were labeled as essential oil education. After getting to know us and our sales pitch free Meetups our group now turns to us as trusted guidance for their Aromatherapy needs.

Before you commit to starting and funding a Meetup Group you have to do your research. Check out the other groups in your area that have an Aromatherapy and essential oil focus. Are they a Multi-Level Marketing company looking to gain sales representatives? Are they a group of individuals that like Aromatherapy but have no formal training? What does each group offer their members? How many group members do they have? How many total Aromatherapy groups are in your area?

This research will help you identify what Meetups you schedule in the future and how you word your Meetup Group information page.

2 GETTING STARTED

As with any group, you want to make sure that you are targeting the group that you want to attract. Meetup will ask you to identify some keywords that people interested in your group may be searching for. This should be relevant to the group but broad enough to encompass groups that may overlap with aromatherapy i.e. holistic health.

Meetup will allow you to choose up to 15 Keywords for your group. They also provide suggestions based on your area and your initial keyword. I suggest starting with the keyword AROMATHERAPY to bring up a more topic specific list. Here are a few of the keywords that I have found to be successful. Remember, choose your keywords based on your area and your Meetup.com research that you did.

Suggested Keywords:

- Aromatherapy
- Holistic Health
- Essential Oils
- Alternative Health and Wellness
- Natural Health
- Complementary and Alternative Medicine
- Improving your health with Aromatherapy
- Essential Oils for Children

Meetup will stop you once you have hit your 15 topic limit. Keep in mind, also, that Meetup.com will automatically invite around 100 individuals in your area to join your Meetup group based on your keywords.

The name of your Meetup group should be relevant to the group of individuals you want to attract. For instance, if you are a Clinical Aromatherapist that specializes in using Aromatherapy for spiritual wellness then a relevant name for your Meetup group may be "Spiritual Aromatherapy Group". Our Meetup group was created with the purpose of including beginners, intermediates, and experienced essential oil users alike. To encompass our vision we chose the name "Triangle Aromatherapy Group". Triangle is specific to our area since we are in the Research Triangle area of North Carolina, and Aromatherapy is a broad term that does not limit us to a certain type of aromatherapy. Again, your Meetup group name must be relevant to the types of classes you will offer.

As an example, let's say that you started the group "Denver Aromatherapy Group". You have several people that sign up for your group at various levels of interest and experience anticipating that this group will be a broad spectrum aromatherapy group. You, however, would like to focus on the spiritual aspect of aromatherapy. After about 2 or 3 Meetups you see that people start to leave the group. Odds are your Meetup group is unhappy with the unintentional "bait and switch". They anticipated an Aromatherapy Group, not a Spiritual Aromatherapy Group.

3 GROUP LOGISTICS

The name of your group may peak potential group members interest but the group description is what helps seal the deal. Group description is also what can get your Meetup group shut down. Learn from my mistakes here.

When Triangle Aromatherapy Group was initially started we wanted to stress that we were not affiliated with any of the multi-level marketing companies and that this group was led by Certified Clinical Aromatherapists. Two weeks later our Meetup group was shut down. I was puzzled. The email that I received from Meetup.com stated that it had been shut down because Meetup does not accept groups that are started as a lead generator for business. I had several email conversations trying to get the situation straightened out but to no avail. I argued that there were several groups with the Multi-Level Marketing company name right in the group name and that we were NOT pushing sales at all. Bottom line is that a new Meetup group is reviewed by a Meetup team member. That team member decides if your group passes the review or not. In the end, I was invited to try again. So I did. Here is the group description that worked for Triangle Aromatherapy Group the second time around. Feel free to use this as a general guideline when starting your Meetup group.

Hello! This is a Meetup group dedicated to bringing together those of us in the Triangle area that love essential oils and aromatherapy and are interested in fellowship, fun, outings, and going to classes with other aromatherapy enthusiasts. Our goal is to bring together novice and experienced alike so that we can all learn from each other and share what we have to offer. You can look forward to a variety of different activities happening in and around the Triangle such as attending workshops, classes, visiting local lavender farms and bee keepers, and sometimes just a dinner out where we can get together and talk essential oils and aromatherapy. Whatever the activity may be, we are excited to have you come along.

Please note, Triangle Aromatherapy Group was started to educated and inspire people on how to use essential oils in their every day lives from the prospective of educated and certified Clinical Aromatherapists, free from the pressures of sales.

We welcome all levels of essential oil enthusiasts; however we do ask that all multi-level marketing reps please refrain from contacting group members in pursuit of sales via the Meetup.com website or at Triangle Aromatherapy Group events.

4 NEW MEMBERS

This is the fun part. What will your Meetup members be called? We call our members "Aromatics". Some other ideas may be "Essential Oil Enthusiasts" or "Spiritual Oilers". Again, make this relevant to your groups direction. Spiritual Oilers would not work for a broad spectrum aromatherapy group.

The next step in creating your Meetup is adding questions for new members. This is not a necessary action to start your Meetup. Triangle Aromatherapy Group asks members two questions when they request to join the group: "What is your level of experience with Aromatherapy" and "What type of classes and events are you interested in". This immediately helps us to identify the experience level of our overall group as well as give us ideas for future Meetups based on what our group members want.

Again, this is optional but I suggest using it to your advantage. As a general rule of thumb, there should be no more than 2 *simple* questions. The goal is not to turn new members away from the group before they finish joining because of an extensive questionnaire.

Another option is to set the questions and uncheck the "Require members to answer these questions" box. This will allow you to offer the questions without mandating they be answered to join. We also found that certain cell phones were not allowing members to join when we made the questions mandatory. After unchecking the required box it has been my experience that very few have bypassed the questions.

After someone joins your Meetup group they will be sent a Welcome Message. This welcome message is set up by you and will be saved to your Meetup group. Meetup then automatically triggers the welcome message to be sent.

The welcome message is a great way to thank a new member for joining your group. It is also a great way to set some foundations and basic ground rules. Below is the welcome letter for Triangle Aromatherapy Group. Feel free to use it as a guideline for your groups objective and needs.

Welcome! We are so excited that you've joined this group. If there's something that you would like to do that is relevant to our group please let us know. We would love to have your ideas for upcoming Meetups!

Triangle Aromatherapy Group was started to educate and inspire people on how to use essential oils in their everyday lives from the prospective of educated and certified Clinical Aromatherapists, free from the pressures of sales.

We welcome all levels of essential oil enthusiasts; however we do ask that all multi-level marketing reps please refrain from contacting group members in pursuit of sales via the Meetup.com website or at Triangle Aromatherapy Group events.

Thank You, and Welcome! We look forward to seeing you soon.

5 YOUR MEETUP INFORMATION

Here is where you let the group know why you are qualified to run this Meetup. Meetup.com will ask you to complete a short bio. If you created questions for your Meetup group to answer upon joining you will also be asked to answer those questions.

Short Bio is key here. You have limited space and not all of the words will show up when you RSVP to a Meetup. Get the most important statement out of the way first. "I am a Certified Clinical Aromatherapist." Expand from there with anything that you feel is relevant to your Meetup profile.

I cannot stress enough how important a photo is. You are a Meetup group owner. This means that people need to know what you look like so that they can find you at events. Your Meetup picture should follow these guidelines:

- Current photo within the last 6 months
- Shows a clear view of your face
- Is an individual photo – not a group photo

You can also require that your members have a photo to join the group. Triangle Aromatherapy Group does not require a photo to join the group. Unfortunately, you cannot control what pictures your group members choose. We have a mixed variety of photos – some have no picture, some have a logo or cartoon instead of a picture, some have multiple people in the picture, some have their children as their picture, some have pictures so old that they are unrecognizable when they show up at the Meetup. This can make it hard on you, as the organizer, to recognize people.

My thought on pictures is this; if a group member feels that their photo is a representation of themselves then I am not the person to judge. I will, however, not search out or wait for a group member at an event that I cannot identify. That, my friends, is like looking for a needle in a haystack.

6 SCHEDULING MEETUPS

The meat and bones of any Meetup group are the scheduled events. There are three things that Triangle Aromatherapy Group has found successful in terms of scheduling:

- A variety of Meetups
- A consistent Meetup schedule
- Advanced scheduling

Let's break these down. A variety of Meetups is important because it shows your members that they won't be hearing the same thing every single Meetup. There is a local Meetup group in my area that has been up and running for 1 year now. They have 20 members in their group. Their group description promises that beginners and experienced natural scent lovers can come together to learn about the hundreds of essential oils that are available. Looking at their schedule of events, however, they only offer Do It Yourself classes such as making a lotion and making a body scrub. When looking at the consistency of scheduling, there are some months that have a Meetup scheduled and some that do not. There are also Meetups that are scheduled without a date and time. These are all deterrents for potential group members. The following formula was successful for Triangle Aromatherapy Group during months 1-6.

2 Meetups minimum per month
One Meetup on a Weekday evening
One Meetup on a Saturday
One Meetup as a DIY Project
One Meetup as a learning discussion
One quarterly personal blending Meetup
Miscellaneous relevant outing i.e. we have a local lavender farm that we went to
Schedule Meetups at a minimum of three months at a time
Keep them around 1 hour each (with the exception of special Meetups that may require more time)

Keep in mind, however, that as your group grows and your core members start to form you may notice a change in what your group is looking for. For instance, as I am writing this it is the end of April. Triangle Aromatherapy Group has Meetups scheduled out through September. During the first six months there was an equal interest between the discussion Meetups and the DIY Meetups. Now that our core group has established Triangle Aromatherapy Group is transitioning into an educational Meetup. The DIY Meetups are losing popularity. This shows that Triangle Aromatherapy Group members want more education now that they have established this group as an information source for their essential oil needs.

This doesn't mean that Triangle Aromatherapy Group will stop offering DIY Meetups. It just means that the number of DIY Meetups will slowly start to be scaled back. Be aware of what your group members are looking for. A successful Meetup group is not a set it and forget it activity.

7 MEETUP MONEY

This, of course, is completely up to you but keep in mind that it typically takes 6 months to a year for your Meetup to really build momentum and pick up speed. At the 6 month mark for Triangle Aromatherapy Group we had 57 members with a core group of around 12 consistent members with an average of 5-8 members per Meetup.

Keeping that in mind, I suggest giving your Meetup at least 6 months to get started.

It costs money to run a Meetup group and some activities will have fees associated with them as well. There are several ways to tackle this with your Meetup group.

- <u>No charge to members</u>
  This one is for the Meetup organizer that doesn't mind footing the bill for everything. It's definitely a bonus for group members since they only need to show up.

- <u>Monthly membership fee</u>
  Some Meetup organizers choose to have a monthly membership fee for their Meetup group. This can work for you or it can work against you. Since there are so many other groups available on Meetup, most people will lean towards the Meetup group that does not charge a monthly fee.

- Per event fee

  This is a pretty popular option on Meetup. Some groups have a policy where they collect $1.00 from each participant at each Meetup event. This typically works better when you have a larger number of group members. Another per event fee is when you hold a specific event that does cost money. For instance, Triangle Aromatherapy Group is having a guest speaker that will be showing the group an essential oil distillation. To cover the costs of the speaker fees Triangle Aromatherapy Group is charging $40.00 per participant.

- Sponsorships

  Sponsorships can be a Meetup organizers best friend financially! Sponsorships come in various forms; free meeting space, member discount, and sometimes financial backing of your group. Some Meetups have a very large number of members which draws sponsors to them. When you are first starting out you will need to do the leg work and seek out sponsorships. Make sure that you know exactly what you are looking for in a sponsor i.e. 6 months of membership fees, free meeting space, etc. and be ready to explain why your group is a good fit for their sponsorship.

- Donation requests

  Another alternative is to offer members the option to donate to the Meetup group. Triangle Aromatherapy Group has found this particularly beneficial for the DIY Meetups. In the Meetup description we state that the Meetup is free but that we do have a suggested donation of $ X.XX to help cover the costs of supplies. At the Meetup we then have a designated jar labeled "DONATIONS" for group members to place their donation. This works because it does not alienate those who may be tight financially and it provides a no pressure environment for group members that may be unsure of paying for an event that they may not be able to make it to.

A combination that works for your group is ideal. Triangle Aromatherapy Group does not charge for the Discussion Meetups, but we do ask a suggested donation for hands on classes that require supplies to be purchased.

I don't know about your area but in my area a decent sized free meeting space is hard to come by. We also have several meeting spaces that are advertised as free but your group has to meet a certain dollar amount of sales, i.e. a local coffee shop here in Raleigh offers a room for free as long as your group has a total of $50.00 in sales during the time that you are using the room. This is a burden on multiple accounts. As a Meetup organizer that means that you may now be shelling out $50.00 for an hour long discussion. This also puts an extra burden on your members by requesting they purchase something. Now your venue has turned into a numbers game instead of you being able to focus on the topic at hand. Not all venues are like this. Some places will offer free meeting spaces, it's just a matter of doing your leg work locally and asking around.

Once your Meetup has been established and you have your core group consider opening the Meetup venues to member homes or your own home. This is a very cost effective way to hold Meetups. One of the great features about Meetup is that you can let group members know that the event will be held at a private residence and then email the address to only the "YES" RSVP's the day before.

8 HANDLING THE "SALES PERSON"

There may come a time when a group member steps outside of the boundaries and you are put in the position of removing them from the group. Triangle Aromatherapy Group has a strict policy that does not allow multi-level marketing sales representatives to approach group members for sales. It is in our group description and in our welcome email. Unfortunately there was a situation where a group member would continuously disrupt Meetups and post to the group message boards about her services and activities outside of Meetup, including her essential oil classes required by her upline representative. A conversation was had and she persisted. An email was sent and she still persisted. It then got to the point where she was banned from the group with an email of explanation sent stating why.

Remember – this is YOUR Meetup group. YOU are the Certified Clinical Aromatherapist with the up to date knowledge and education. Don't be afraid to ban someone from your group that has proven to be a threat to the integrity of what you offer your group members.

9 WORKSHEETS

Starting a Meetup group can be one of the most rewarding decisions you make as a Clinical Aromatherapist and Business Owner. It not only places you as the expert, it gives you exposure to individuals and potential clients consistently.

Use the worksheets on the following pages to help you get organized and ready to start your Meetup.

Creating a Meetup Group – Getting Started

Goal and Focus of Meetup Group: _____

_____

_____

_____

_____

_____

_____

Group Name: _____

_____

Members will be called: _____

_____

Potential Sponsors: _____

_____

_____

_____

_____

Meetup Planner

Date of Meetup: _____

Time of Meetup: _____

Venue: _____

Charge for Meetup: _____

Supplies needed: _____

_____

_____

_____

_____

Cost of Supplies: _____

_____

_____

Handouts: _____

_____

_____

_____

6 Month Meetup Schedule

Month			
Day and Time			
Topic			
Materials Needed			
Venue			
Charge			
Handouts Needed			
Misc.			

Month			
Day and Time			
Topic			
Materials Needed			
Venue			
Charge			
Handouts Needed			
Misc.			

Month			
Day and Time			
Topic			
Materials Needed			
Venue			
Charge			
Handouts Needed			
Misc.			

Month			
Day and Time			
Topic			
Materials Needed			
Venue			
Charge			
Handouts Needed			
Misc.			

MANDY SAVARD

ABOUT THE AUTHOR

Mandy Savard is a nationally recognized Business Development Coach and  founder of Clinical Alchemy. She has a genius for helping New and Seasoned Aromatherapists create a practice that allows them to thrive and prosper while doing what they love.

Graduate Degree in Organizational Leadership, Coaching Certification from ICF accredited Coach Training Alliance, and Certification in Clinical Aromatherapy as well as the experience of starting successful businesses in both the nonprofit and for profit sectors; Mandy helps Aromatherapists to achieve their goals of working for themselves on an everyday basis. Her easy to implement entrepreneur strategies start you off on the fast track to success.

Her insightful website – www.clinicalalchemy.com – offers resources and a sign up area for Inspiration and Business Tip emails. Share your questions, opinions, and ideas on her website at any time. Mandy would love to meet you and find out about the unique business ideas that will take you to the next level.

www.ingramcontent.com/pod-product-compliance
Lightning Source LLC
Chambersburg PA
CBHW070730180526
45167CB00004B/1693